Ten Little Ducks

WRITTEN AND ILLUSTRATED BY

Franklin Hammond

For Quinn

A Meadow Mouse Paperback
Groundwood/Douglas & McIntyre
Toronto/Vancouver

1 One

One little duck in the drizzling rain,
plip, plop, drip, drop.

2 Two

Two little ducks jump in a puddle,
stamp, splash, splish, squish.

3 Three

Three little ducks waddle in the door,
squelch, squirt, slip, trip.

4 Four

Four little ducks mop and shine the floor,
wash, swoosh, swash, swish.

5 Five

Five little ducks at a lemon-tea party,
sip, slurp, clink, drink.

6 Six

Six little ducks scrubbing in the tub,
gurgle, glub, bubble, rub.

7   Seven

Seven little ducks brush and buff their beaks,
clean, squeak, shine, beam.

8 Eight

Eight little ducks cosy in pajamas,
warm and snug as bugs in rugs.

9 Nine

Nine little ducks read favorite bedtime stories,
droop, wink, stretch, blink.

10 Ten

Ten little ducks carry teddy bears upstairs,
yawn, cuddle, squeeze, snuggle.

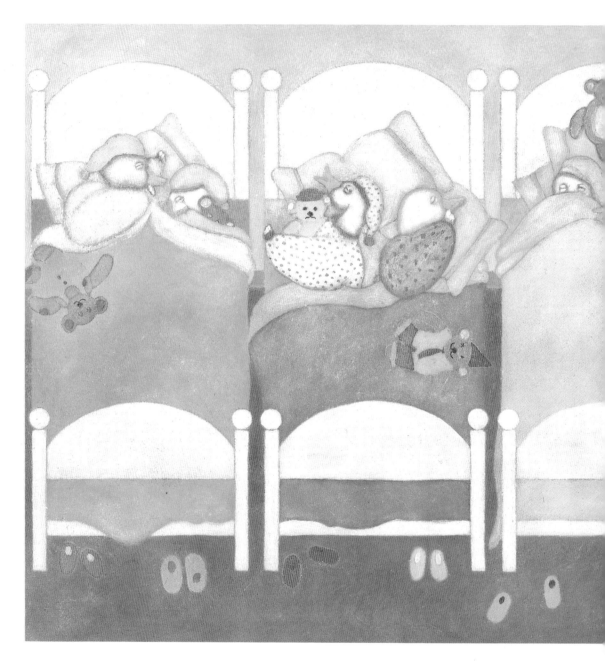

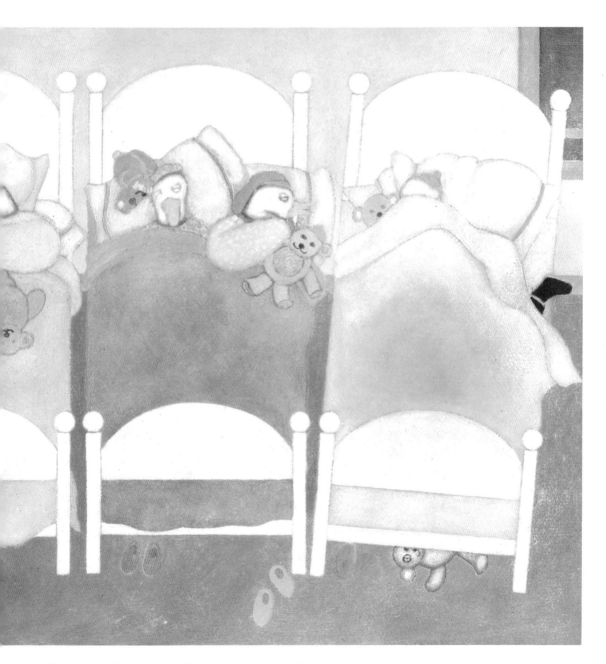

All the little ducks tucked up in their beds,
drowse, and dream, and sleep.

Goodnight.

Copyright ©1987 by Franklin Hammond
Meadow Mouse Paperback edition 1992
Second printing 1992

A Meadow Mouse Paperback
Douglas & McIntyre Ltd.
585 Bloor Street West
Toronto, Ontario   M6G 1K5

Canadian Cataloguing in Publication Data

Hammond, Franklin
  Ten little ducks

"A Meadow mouse paperback".
ISBN 0-88899-153-3

1. Counting – Juvenile literature. I. Title.

QA113.H36 1992   j513.2'11   C91-095302-3

Design by Michael Solomon
Printed in Hong Kong